Table of Contents

100
words every
word lover
should know

THE **100** WORDS ® *From the Editors of the*
AMERICAN HERITAGE®
DICTIONARIES

HOUGHTON MIFFLIN
Boston   New York

Visit our websites: www.ahdictionary.com
or www.houghtonmifflinbooks.com

ISBN-13: 978-0-618-55146-0
ISBN-10: 0-618-55146-8

LIBRARY OF CONGRESS CATALOGING-IN-PUBLICATION DATA

100 words every word lover should know : the 100 words /
from the editors of the American Heritage dictionaries.
   p. cm.
 ISBN 0-618-55146-8
 1. English language -- Etymology.   2. Vocabulary.   I. Title:
One hundred words every word lover should know.
   PE1574.A14 2005
   422 -- dc22

                                                    2004023109

Text design by Anne Chalmers

MANUFACTURED IN THE UNITED STATES OF AMERICA

QUM 10 9 8 7 6 5

Preface

The editors of the *American Heritage* dictionaries are pleased to present the fourth book in our "100 Words" series, *100 Words Every Word Lover Should Know*. Every lover of the English language will enjoy the rich panoply of words, from *aesthetic* to *zenith*, that are on display.

Entries are based on the content of the *American Heritage* dictionaries and are presented in an expanded layout that is easy to read and comprehend. The staff of the *American Heritage* dictionaries selected the words in this book for a variety of reasons. Many items, such as *chortle* and *internecine,* have an interesting history; accompanying these words are notes that explain the story of their development. Other words are associated with interesting facts; see, for example, *facetious.* Still other words are staff favorites because of how they sound (*humuhumunukunukuapuaa*) or what they mean (*koan*).

Additionally, we show the use of many words in context by printing over 75 quotations from a wide mix of classical novelists (Nathaniel Hawthorne, *The House of the Seven Gables*; Charlotte Brontë, *Jane Eyre*), familiar 20th-century novelists (Sylvia Plath, *The Bell Jar*; Shirley Jackson, *The Haunting of Hill House*), contemporary authors (Laura Hillenbrand, *Seabiscuit*; Donna

Tartt, *The Secret History*), and current columnists and contributors to popular periodicals and newspapers (Wendy Kaminer, *Atlantic Monthly*; Gary Stix, *Scientific American*). These quotations show that these are not only words that word lovers should know, they're also ones that word lovers actually *use*.

The first three books in the "100 Words" series, *100 Words Every High School Graduate Should Know, 100 Words Every High School Freshman Should Know*, and *100 Words Almost Everyone Confuses and Misuses*, have generated immense interest. We remain delighted by the enthusiastic response to these books and are encouraged by the fact that so many people are taking a strong interest in using dictionaries as an integral part of literacy and vocabulary building. We hope that you will have as much fun reading *100 Words Every Word Lover Should Know* as we did in compiling this book.

— Steve Kleinedler,
Senior Editor

Guide to the Entries

THIS GUIDE EXPLAINS THE CONVENTIONS
USED IN THIS BOOK.

ENTRY WORD The 100 words that constitute this book
are listed alphabetically. The entry words, along with
inflected and derived forms, are divided into syllables
by centered dots. These dots show you where you
would break the word at the end of a line. The pronunciation of the word follows the entry word. Please see
the key on page xi for an explanation of the pronunciation system.

PART OF SPEECH At least one part of speech follows
each entry word. The part of speech tells you the grammatical category that the word belongs to. Parts of
speech include *noun*, *adjective*, *adverb*, *transitive verb*,
and *intransitive verb*. (A transitive verb is a verb that
needs an object to complete its meaning. *Wash* is a
transitive verb in the sentence *I washed the car*. The di-
rect object of *wash* is *the car*. An intransitive verb is one
that does not take an object, as *sleep* in the sentence *I
slept for seven hours*. Many verbs are both transitive and
intransitive.)

INFLECTIONS A word's inflected forms differ from the
main entry form by the addition of a suffix or by a

---

change in the base form to indicate grammatical features such as number, person, or tense. They are set in boldface type, divided into syllables, and given pronunciations as necessary. The past tense, past participle, and the third person singular present tense inflections of all verbs are shown. The plurals of nouns are shown when they are spelled in a way other than by adding *s* to the base form.

ORDER OF SENSES Entries having more than one sense are arranged with the central and often the most commonly sought meanings first. In an entry with more than one part of speech, the senses are numbered in separate sequences after each part of speech, as at **halcyon.**

EXAMPLES OF USAGE Examples often follow the definitions and are set in italic type. These examples show the entry words in typical contexts. Sometimes the examples are quotations from authors of books. These quotations are shown within quotation marks, and the quotation's author and source are shown in parentheses.

ETYMOLOGIES Etymologies appear in square brackets following the last definition. An etymology traces the history of a word as far back in time as can be determined with reasonable certainty. The stage most closely preceding Modern English is given first, with each earlier stage following in sequence. A language name, linguistic form (in italics), and brief definition of the form are given for each stage of the derivation. To avoid redundancy, a language, form, or definition is not repeated if it is identical to the corresponding item in the immediately preceding stage. Occasionally, a form will be given that is not actually preserved in written documents but which scholars are confident did exist—such a form will be marked by an asterisk (*). The word *from* is used to indicate origin of any kind: by inheritance, borrowing, or derivation. When an etymology splits a compound word into parts, a colon introduces the parts and each element is then traced back to its origin, with those elements enclosed in parentheses.

NOTES Many entries include Notes that present interesting information regarding the history of the word, including the process by which it entered English from other languages.

Pronunciation Guide

Pronunciations appear in parentheses after boldface entry words. If a word has more than one pronunciation, the first pronunciation is usually more common than the other, but often they are equally common. Pronunciations are shown after inflections and related words where necessary.

Stress is the relative degree of emphasis that a word's syllables are spoken with. An unmarked syllable has the weakest stress in the word. The strongest, or primary, stress is indicated with a bold mark (ˈ). A lighter mark (ʹ) indicates a secondary level of stress. The stress mark follows the syllable it applies to. Words of one syllable have no stress mark because there is no other stress level that the syllable can be compared to.

The key on page xi shows the pronunciation symbols used in this book. To the right of the symbols are words that show how the symbols are pronounced. The letters whose sound corresponds to the symbols are shown in boldface.

The symbol (ə) is called *schwa*. It represents a vowel with the weakest level of stress in a word. The schwa sound varies slightly according to the vowel it represents or the sounds around it:

a·bun·dant (ə-bŭnʹdənt)   **mo·ment** (mōʹmənt)

civ·il (sĭvʹəl)   **grate·ful** (grātʹfəl)

PRONUNCIATION KEY

Symbol	Examples	Symbol	Examples
ă	pat	oi	noise
ā	pay	o͝o	took
âr	care	o͝or	lure
ä	father	o͞o	boot
b	bib	ou	out
ch	church	œ	*German* schön
d	deed, milled	p	pop
ĕ	pet	r	roar
ē	bee	s	sauce
f	fife, phase, rough	sh	ship, dish
		t	tight, stopped
g	gag	th	thin
h	hat	*th*	this
hw	which	ŭ	cut
ĭ	pit	ûr	urge, term, firm, word, heard
ī	pie, by		
îr	deer, pier		
j	judge	v	valve
k	kick, cat, pique	w	with
l	lid, needle	y	yes
m	mum	z	zebra, xylem
n	no, sudden	zh	vision, pleasure, garage
N	*French* bon		
ng	thing		
ŏ	pot	ə	about, item, edible, gallop, circus
ō	toe		
ô	caught, paw		
ôr	core	ər	butter

To visit one's lover, with tears and reproaches, at his own residence, was an image so agreeable to Mrs. Penniman's mind that she felt a sort of **aesthetic** disappointment at its lacking, in this case, the harmonious accompaniments of darkness and storm. A quiet Sunday afternoon appeared an inadequate setting for it; and, indeed, Mrs. Penniman was quite out of humour with the conditions of the time, which passed very slowly as she sat in the front-parlour, in her bonnet and her cashmere shawl, awaiting Catherine's return.

— Henry James,
Washington Square

aes·thet·ic or es·thet·ic (ĕs-thĕt′ĭk)

adjective

1. Relating to beauty or the appreciation of beauty: *"To visit one's lover, with tears and reproaches, at his own residence, was an image so agreeable to Mrs. Penniman's mind that she felt a sort of aesthetic disappointment at its lacking, in this case, the harmonious accompaniments of darkness and storm"* (Henry James, *Washington Square*).
2. Exhibiting beauty; pleasing in appearance: *The new website features a number of aesthetic enhancements.*
3. Relating to the branch of philosophy that deals with the nature and expression of beauty, as in the fine arts.

noun

A conception of what is artistically valid or beautiful: *The aesthetics of Modernism can be seen as a reaction to the staid conventions of Victorian culture.*

[German *ästhetisch,* from New Latin *aesthēticus,* from Greek *aisthētikos,* of sense perception, from *aisthēta,* perceptible things, from *aisthanesthai,* to perceive.]

al·che·my (ăl′kə-mē)

noun

1. A medieval chemical philosophy having as its asserted aims the transmutation of base metals into gold, the discovery of the panacea, and the preparation of the elixir of longevity. **2.** A seemingly magical power or process of transmuting: *"He wondered by what alchemy it* [a killed deer] *was changed, so that what sickened him one hour, maddened him with hunger the next"* (Marjorie K. Rawlings, *The Yearling*).

[Middle English *alkamie,* from Old French *alquemie,* from Medieval Latin *alchymia,* from Arabic *al-kīmiyā'* : *al-,* the + *kīmiyā',* chemistry (from Late Greek *khēmeia, khumeia,* perhaps from Greek *Khēmia,* Egypt).]

al·le·go·ry (ăl′ĭ-gôr′ē)

noun
Plural: **al·le·go·ries**

1a. The representation of abstract ideas or principles by characters, figures, or events in narrative, dramatic, or pictorial form. **b.** A story, picture, or play employing such representation. John Bunyan's *Pilgrim's Progress* and Herman Melville's *Moby-Dick* are allegories. **2.** A symbolic representation: *The blindfolded figure with scales is an allegory of justice.*

[Middle English *allegorie,* from Latin *allēgoria,* from Greek, from *allēgorein,* to interpret allegorically : *allos,* other + *agoreuein,* to speak publicly (from *agorā,* marketplace).]

a·nach·ro·nism (ə-năk**ʹ**rə-nĭz**ʹ**əm)

noun

1. The representation of someone as existing or something as happening in other than chronological, proper, or historical order. **2.** One that is out of its proper or chronological order, especially a person or practice that belongs to an earlier time: *"A new age had plainly dawned, an age that made the institution of a segregated picnic seem an anachronism"* (Henry Louis Gates, Jr., *Colored People: A Memoir*). *"Cavalry regiments of cuirassiers with glistening metal breastplates and long black horsehair tails hanging down from their helmets were conscious of no anachronism. Following them came huge crates housing airplanes and wheeled platforms bearing the long narrow gray-painted field guns, the* soixante-quinzes *that were France's pride"* (Barbara W. Tuchman, *The Guns of August*).

[French *anachronisme,* from New Latin *anachronismus,* from Late Greek *anakhronismos,* from *anakhronizesthai,* to be an anachronism : Greek *ana-,* up, backward + Greek *khronizein,* to take time (from *khronos,* time).]

a·nath·e·ma (ə-năth′ə-mə)

noun

  Plural: **a·nath·e·mas**

1. An ecclesiastical ban, curse, or excommunication. **2.** A vehement denunciation or curse: *"If the children gathered about her . . . Pearl would grow positively terrible in her puny wrath, snatching up stones to fling at them, with shrill, incoherent exclamations that made her mother tremble, because they had so much the sound of a witch's anathemas in some unknown tongue"* (Nathaniel Hawthorne, *The Scarlet Letter*). **3.** One that is cursed or damned. **4.** One that is greatly reviled, loathed, or shunned: *"Essentialism—a belief in natural, immutable sex differences—is anathema to postmodernists, for whom sexuality itself, along with gender, is a 'social construct'"*(Wendy Kaminer, *Atlantic Monthly*).

[Late Latin *anathema,* accursed thing, from Greek, something dedicated, something devoted (to evil), from *anatithenai, anathe-,* to dedicate : *ana-,* up, backward- + *tithenai,* to put.]

---

bail·i·wick (bā′lə-wĭk′)

noun

1. A person's specific area of interest, skill, or authority: *"Tower liked people to be like himself: quick, sharp and to the point. A private school and a restricted cruise were his natural bailiwicks"* (Louis Auchincloss, "The Atonement"). **2.** The office or district of a bailiff: *"Another writ has been issued . . . and the defendant in that cause is the prey of the sheriff having legal jurisdiction in this bailiwick"* (Charles Dickens, *David Copperfield*).

[Middle English *bailliwik* : *baillif*, bailiff (ultimately from Latin *bāiulus*, carrier) + *wik*, town (from Old English *wīc*, from Latin *vīcus*).]

be·lea·guered (bĭ-lē′gərd)

adjective

1. Beset with troubles or problems: *"The beleaguered rider could do no better than cling to the horse's neck for dear life"* (Laura Hillenbrand, *Seabiscuit*). **2.** Surrounded with troops; besieged.

[Probably Dutch *belegeren* (*be-*, around + *leger,* camp) + *-ed,* past participle suffix.]

Seabiscuit didn't run, he rampaged. When the rider . . . tried to rein him in, the horse bolted, thrashing around like a hooked marlin. Asked to go left, he'd dodge right; tugged right, he'd dart left. The **beleaguered** rider could do no better than cling to the horse's neck for dear life.

— Laura Hillenbrand,
Seabiscuit

bro·mide (brō′mīd′)

noun

1a. A binary compound of bromine with another element, such as silver. **b.** Potassium bromide, a white crystalline solid or powder used as a sedative, in photographic emulsion, and in lithography. **2a.** A commonplace remark or notion; a platitude: *"The windows of buses and shops were adorned with bromides: 'The only magic to remove poverty—hard work, clear vision, iron will, strict discipline'"*(Katherine Frank, *Indira: The Life of Indira Nehru Gandhi*). **b.** A tiresome person; a bore.

[From *bromine* (from French *brome*, from Greek *brōmos*, stench + *-ine*, suffix used in names of chemical substances) + *-ide*, suffix in names of chemical compounds.]

☙ Several bromine compounds, especially potassium bromide, have been used medicinally as sedatives. In 1906 Gelett Burgess (the coiner of the word *blurb*) wrote a book entitled *Are You a Bromide?* in which he used *bromide* to mean a tiresome person of unoriginal thoughts and trite conversation, the sort of person who might put you to sleep. *Bromide* was soon after extended to include the kind of commonplace remarks that could be expected from a bromide, such as "You're a sight for sore eyes."

cap·puc·ci·no (kăp′ə-chē′nō, kä′pə-chē′nō)

noun
>   Plural: **cap·puc·ci·nos**

Espresso coffee mixed or topped with steamed milk or cream.

[Italian, Capuchin, cappuccino (from the resemblance of its color to the color of the monk's habit).]

℘ The history of the word *cappuccino* shows how words can de-velop new senses because of resemblances that the original coiners of the terms might not have dreamed possible. The Ital-ian name of the Capuchin order of friars, established after 1525, came from the long pointed cowl, or *cappuccino,* that was worn as part of the order's habit. In Italian *cappuccino* went on to de-velop another sense, "espresso coffee mixed or topped with steamed milk or cream," probably because the color of the cof-fee resembled the color of the habit of a Capuchin friar.

ca·price (kə-prēs′)

noun

1a. An impulsive change of mind. **b.** An inclination to change one's mind impulsively. **c.** A sudden, unpredictable action, change, or series of actions or changes: *". . . six hours of alert immobility while the boat drove slowly or floated arrested, according to the caprice of the wind"* (Joseph Conrad, *Lord Jim*). **2.** *Music* An instrumental work with an improvisatory style and a free form; a capriccio.

[French, from Italian *capriccio,* from *caporiccio,* fright, sudden start : *capo,* head (from Latin *caput*) + *riccio,* curly (from Latin *ēricius,* hedgehog, from *ēr*).]

11

car·i·bou (kăr′ə-bōō′)

noun
    Plural: **caribou** *or* **car·i·bous**

Any of several large reindeer native to northern North
America.

[Micmac *ĝalipu* (influenced by Canadian French *caribou*,
also from Micmac), from Proto-Algonquin **mekālixpowa* :
*mekāl-, to scrape + **-ixpo-*, snow.]

12

chi·as·mus (kī-ăz′məs)

noun
    Plural: **chi·as·mi** (kī-ăz′mī′)

A rhetorical inversion of the second of two parallel
structures, as in *"Each throat / Was parched, and glazed
each eye"* (Samuel Taylor Coleridge, *The Rime of the
Ancient Mariner*).

[New Latin *chīasmus,* from Greek *khīasmos,* syntactic inversion, from *khīazein,* to invert or mark with an X.]

chor·tle (chôr′tl)

noun

A snorting, joyful laugh or chuckle.

intransitive and transitive verb
    Past participle and past tense: **chor·tled**
    Present participle: **chor·tling**
    Third person singular present tense: **chor·tles**

To utter a chortle or express with a chortle.

[Blend of *chuckle* and *snort.*]

Ɉ␥ "'O frabjous day! Callooh! Callay!' He chortled in his joy." Perhaps Lewis Carroll would chortle a bit himself to find that people are still using the word *chortle,* which he coined in *Through the Looking-Glass,* published in 1872. In any case, Carroll had constructed his word well, combining the words *chuckle* and *snort.* This type of word is called a *blend* or a *portmanteau word.* In *Through the Looking-Glass* Humpty Dumpty uses *portmanteau* ("a large leather suitcase that opens into two hinged compartments") to describe the word *slithy,* saying, "It's like a portmanteau — there are two meanings packed up into one word" (the meanings being "lithe" and "slimy").

14
coc·cyx (kŏk′sĭks)

noun
    Plural: **coc·cy·ges** (kŏk-sī′jēz, kŏk′sĭ-jēz′)

A small triangular bone at the base of the spinal column in humans and tailless apes, consisting of several fused rudimentary vertebrae. Also called *tailbone.*

[New Latin *coccȳx,* from Greek *kokkūx,* cuckoo, coccyx (from its resemblance to a cuckoo's beak).]

cres·cen·do (krə-shĕn′dō)

noun

Plural: **cres·cen·dos** *or* **cres·cen·di** (krə-shĕn′dē)

1. *Music* **a.** A gradual increase, especially in the volume or intensity of sound in a passage. **b.** A passage played with a gradual increase in volume or intensity. **2.** A steady increase in intensity or force: "*Then the sound came, a long, deep, powerful rumble increasing in crescendo until the windows rattled, cups danced in their saucers, and the bar glasses rubbed rims and tinkled in terror. The sound slowly ebbed, then boomed to a fiercer climax, closer*" (Pat Frank, *Alas, Babylon*).

intransitive verb

Past participle and past tense: **cres·cen·doed**
Present participle: **cres·cen·do·ing**
Third person singular present tense: **cres·cen·does**

To build up to a point of great intensity, force, or volume.

[Italian, present participle of *crescere*, to increase, from Latin *crēscere*.]

cru·ci·ver·bal·ist (krōō′sə-vûr′bə-lĭst)

noun

1. A person who constructs crosswords. **2.** An enthusiast of word games, especially of crosswords.

[From Latin *crux, cruc-*, cross + Latin *verbum,* word (translation of English *crossword*).]

des·ul·to·ry (dĕs′əl-tôr′ē, dĕz′əl-tôr′ē)

adjective

1. Having no set plan; haphazard or random: *"[These] concert series, done mostly on a shoestring and involving many refugee musicians . . . were a beacon of enterprise on the desultory wartime musical scene"* (Meirion Bowen, *BBC Music Magazine*). **2.** Moving or jumping from one thing to another; disconnected: *"She had suddenly begun speaking, after sitting silently through several hours of desultory discussion with her husband about the Resistance"* (Adam Nossiter, *The Algeria Hotel*). *"Our conversation so far had been desultory, with lots of long silences and me staring fixedly out the window"* (Scott Anderson, *Men's Journal*).

[Latin *dēsultōrius,* leaping, from *dēsultor,* a leaper, from *dēsultus,* past participle of *dēsilīre,* to leap down : *dē-*, off + *salīre,* to jump.]

18
de·tri·tus (dĭ-trī′təs)

noun
Plural: **detritus**

1. Loose fragments or grains that have been worn away from rock. **2.** Disintegrated or eroded matter; debris: *Archaeologists study the detritus of past civilizations.*

[French *détritus,* from Latin *dētrītus,* from past participle of *dēterere,* to lessen, wear away.]

19
didj·er·i·doo *or* **didg·er·i·doo**
(dĭj′ə-rē-do͞o′, dĭj′ə-rē-do͞o′)

noun
Plural: **didj·er·i·doos** *or* **didg·er·i·doos**

A musical instrument of the Aboriginal peoples of Australia, consisting of a long hollow branch or stick that makes a deep drone when blown into while vibrating the lips.

[Imitative of its sound.]

e·bul·lient (ĭ-bool′yənt′)

adjective

1. Zestfully enthusiastic: *"She was one of those intensely ebullient people who are great at the right kind of party but wearing in a small space"* (Deirdre McNamer, *My Russian*). **2.** Boiling or seeming to boil; bubbling.

[Latin *ēbulliēns, ēbullient-*, present participle of *ēbullīre*, to bubble up : *ē-, ex-*, out, away + *bullīre*, to bubble, boil.]

ech·e·lon (ĕsh′ə-lŏn′)

noun

1a. A formation of troops in which each unit is positioned successively to the left or right of the rear unit to form an oblique or steplike line. **b.** A flight formation or arrangement of craft in this manner. **c.** A similar formation of groups, units, or individuals: *"By asking the right questions and choosing the right tests and drawing the right conclusions the mechanic works his way down the echelons of the motorcycle hierarchy until he has found the exact specific cause or causes of the engine failure, and then he changes them so that they no longer cause the failure"* (Robert Pirsig, *Zen and the Art of Motorcycle Maintenance*). **2.** A subdivision of a military or naval force. **3.** A level of responsibility or authority in a hierarchy; a rank: *The recent graduate took a job in the company's lower echelon.*

[French *échelon*, from Old French *eschelon*, rung of a ladder, from *eschiele*, ladder, from Late Latin *scāla*, back-formation from Latin *scālae*, steps, ladder.]

22

e·gre·gious (ĭ-grē′jəs, ĭ-grē′jē-əs)

adjective

Conspicuously bad or offensive: *"This is a difficult chapter for me to write—not because my own youthful mistakes were so egregious . . . but because I may be making a mistake now"* (Wendy Lesser, *Nothing Remains the Same: Rereading and Remembering*).

[From Latin *ēgregius,* outstanding : *ē-, ex-,* out, away + *grex, greg-,* herd.]

23

e·phem·er·al (ĭ-fĕm′ər-əl)

adjective

1. Lasting for a markedly brief time: *"There remain some truths too ephemeral to be captured in the cold pages of a court transcript"* (Irving R. Kaufman, *New York Times Magazine*). *"Despite his position, Shah Zaman smiled like the Genie through his pearly beard and declared that Scheherazade was right to think love ephemeral. But life itself was scarcely less so, and both were sweet for just that reason—sweeter yet when enjoyed as if they might endure"* (John Barth, *Chimera*). **2.** Living or lasting only for a day, as certain plants or insects do.

noun

Something that is markedly short-lived.

[From Greek *ephēmeros* : *ep-, epi-,* upon, during + *hēmerā,* day.]

ep·i·cure (ĕp′ĭ-kyŏŏr′)

noun

1. A person with refined taste, especially in food and wine. **2.** A person devoted to sensuous pleasure and luxurious living.

[Middle English, an Epicurean, from Medieval Latin *epicūrus*, from Latin *Epicūrus*, Latin form of the name of *Epikouros*, Greek philosopher (341–270 BC) who advocated the pursuit of pleasure enjoyed in moderation.]

er·satz (ĕr′zäts′, ĕr-zäts′)

adjective

Being an imitation or a substitute, usually an inferior one; artificial: *"Now when she flips through memories, they have an ersatz quality, the sort of tint applied to enhance photos"* (Carol Anshaw, *Seven Moves*).

[German, replacement, from *ersetzen,* to replace, from Old High German *irsezzan* : *ir-,* out + *sezzan,* to set.]

Chris is not sure anymore who it is she's searching for. Now that the person she loved turns out to have been in great part concocted for her approval, who she is missing and who she might find are quite different people. Now when she flips through memories, they have an **ersatz** quality, the sort of tint applied to enhance photos—rose on the cheeks of the sallow graduate, blue on the muddy lake of the dilapidated resort.

—Carol Anshaw,
Seven Moves

26

fa·ce·tious (fə-sē′shəs)

adjective

Playfully jocular; humorous: *"He pointed out—writing in a foolish, facetious tone—that the perfection of mechanical appliances must ultimately supersede limbs"* (H.G. Wells, *The War of the Worlds*). *"[A]unty gave George a nudge with her finger, designed to be immensely facetious, and turned again to her griddle with great briskness"* (Harriet Beecher Stowe, *Uncle Tom's Cabin*).

[French *facétieux*, from *facétie*, jest, from Latin *facētia*, from *facētus*, witty.]

❧ *Facetious* is one of a very small number of English words that contain all five vowels in alphabetical order. (Another is *abstemious*.) The adverb *facetiously* contains all the vowels and *y* in order.

fe·cun·di·ty (fĭ-kŭn′dĭ-tē)

noun

1. The quality or power of producing abundantly; fruitfulness or fertility: *"In the Permian and Triassic periods, what is now the continent of Europe was dominated by endless sandy wastes, blasted by hot dry winds. Lifelessness, aridity and blistering heat suddenly took the place of all that Carboniferous moisture and fecundity"* (Simon Winchester, *The Map That Changed the World*).
2. Productive or creative power: *fecundity of the mind.*

[From *fecund* (from Middle English, from Old French *fecond,* from Latin *fēcundus,* fertile, fruitful) + *-ity,* noun-forming suffix.]

fo·cac·ci·a
(fə-kä′chē′ə, fō-kä′chē′ə, fō-kä′chə)

noun

A flat Italian bread traditionally flavored with olive oil and salt and often topped with herbs, onions, or other items.

[Italian, hearth-cake, from Late Latin *focācia,* of the hearth, feminine of *focācius,* from Latin *focus,* hearth.]

fus·ty (fŭs′tē)

adjective

 Comparative: **fus·ti·er**
 Superlative: **fus·ti·est**

1. Smelling of mildew or decay; musty *"goggle-eyed headlines staring up at me on every street corner and at the fusty, peanut-smelling mouth of every subway"* (Sylvia Plath, *The Bell Jar*). **2.** Old-fashioned; antique.

[Middle English, from Old French *fust,* piece of wood, wine cask, from Latin *fūstis,* stick, club.]

It was a queer, sultry summer, the summer they electrocuted the Rosenbergs, and I didn't know what I was doing in New York. I'm stupid about executions. The idea of being electrocuted makes me sick, and that's all there was to read about in the papers — goggle-eyed headlines staring up at me on every street corner and at the **fusty,** peanut-smelling mouth of every subway. It had nothing to do with me, but I couldn't help wondering what it would be like, being burned alive all along your nerves.

— Sylvia Plath,
The Bell Jar

30 ge·müt·lich·keit

(gə-mōot′lĭk-kīt′, gə-müt′lĭкн-kīt′)

noun

Warm friendliness; amicability.

[German *gemütlich*, congenial (from Middle High German *gemüetlich*, from *gemüete*, spirit, feelings, from Old High German *gimuoti*, from *muot*, mind, spirit, joy) + *-keit*, -ness.]

31 glos·so·la·li·a

(glô′sə-lā′lē-ə, glŏs′ə-lā′lē-ə)

noun

1. Fabricated and nonmeaningful speech, especially such speech associated with a trance state or certain schizophrenic syndromes. **2.** The ability or phenomenon to utter words or sounds of a language unknown to the speaker, especially as an expression of religious ecstasy. In this sense, also called *gift of tongues, speaking in tongues.*

[New Latin : Greek *glōssa*, tongue + Greek *lalein*, to babble.]

gos·sa·mer (gŏs′ə-mər)

adjective

1. Sheer, light, and delicate: *"[F]rom the looping cascades of communication and control emerge the particular parts of a body in perfect form, nearly every time: the needle nose of the narwhal, the gossamer wing of a butterfly, . . . the marvelous globe of the human eye somehow ready upon arrival out of a dark world instantly to receive light"* (Jennifer Ackerman, *Chance in the House of Fate*). **2.** Tenuous; flimsy: *"He knew he was in trouble, but the trouble was glamorous, and he surrounded it with the gossamer lie of make-believe. He was living the storybook legend"* (Evan Hunter, "First Offense").

noun

1. A soft sheer gauzy fabric. **2.** Something delicate, light, or flimsy. **3.** A fine film of cobwebs often seen floating in the air or caught on bushes or grass.

[Middle English *gossomer* : *gos,* goose + *somer,* summer (probably from the abundance of gossamer during early autumn when geese are in season).]

33
gra·va·men (grə-vā**ʹ**mən)

noun
    Plural **gra·va·mens** *or*
    gra·vam·i·na (grə-văm**ʹ**ə-nə)

The part of a legal charge or an accusation that weighs most substantially against the accused.

[Medieval Latin *gravāmen,* injury, accusation, from Late Latin, encumbrance, obligation, from Latin *gravāre,* to burden, from *gravis,* heavy.]

34

hal·cy·on (hăl′sē-ən)

adjective

1. Calm and peaceful; tranquil: *"[I]t was the most halcyon summer I ever spent. We walked the river in the daytime, talking and watching and listening and holding hands, sitting in the dust, in the cool shade beneath the big oaks, and just listening to the mourning doves"* (Rick Bass, *The Sky, the Stars, the Wilderness*). **2.** Prosperous; golden: *"There is probably hardly a single American who does not yearn for a return to the halcyon years of the Eisenhower and Kennedy presidencies, when American manufacturers paid the highest wages in the world yet nonetheless almost effortlessly dominated world markets"* (Eammon Fingleton, *In Praise of Hard Industries*).

noun

1. A kingfisher, especially one of the genus *Halcyon*. **2.** A fabled bird, identified with the kingfisher, that was supposed to have had the power to calm the wind and the waves while it nested on the sea during the winter solstice.

[Middle English *alcioun,* from Latin *alcyōn, halcyōn,* from Greek *halkuōn,* a mythical bird, kingfisher, alteration (influenced by *hals,* salt, sea, and *kuōn,* conceiving, becoming pregnant) of *alkuōn.*]

They found a piglet caught in a curtain of creepers, throwing itself at the elastic traces in all the madness of extreme terror. . . . The three boys rushed forward and Jack drew his knife again with a flourish. He raised his arm in the air. There came a pause, a **hiatus,** the pig continued to scream and the creepers to jerk, and the blade continued to flash at the end of a bony arm. The pause was only long enough for them to understand what an enormity the downward stroke would be.

—William Golding,
Lord of the Flies

35
hi·a·tus (hī-ā′təs)

noun
    Plural: **hi·a·tus·es** *or* **hiatus**

1. A gap or interruption in space, time, or continuity; a break: *"There came a pause, a hiatus, the pig continued to scream and the creepers to jerk, and the blade continued to flash at the end of a bony arm"* (William Golding, *The Lord of the Flies*). **2.** A slight pause that occurs when two immediately adjacent vowels in consecutive syllables are pronounced, as in *reality* and *naïve.* **3.** A separation, aperture, fissure, or short passage in an organ or part of the body.

[Latin *hiātus,* from past participle of *hiāre,* to gape.]

hu·mu·hu·mu·nu·ku·nu·ku·a·pu·a·a

(hōō′mōō-hōō′mōō-nōō′kōō-nōō′kōō-ä′pōō-ä′ä′)

noun

Plural: **humuhumunukunukuapuaa** *or*
hu·mu·hu·mu·nu·ku·nu·ku·a·pu·a·as

Either of two triggerfishes, *Rhinecanthus aculeatus* or *R. rectangulus,* native to the outer reefs of Hawaii, the latter having a broad black band on the side and a black triangle at the beginning of the tail. The humuhumunukunukuapuaa is the state fish of Hawaii.

[Hawaiian *humuhumu-nukunuku-ā-pua'a,* trigger fish with
a blunt snout like a pig's : *humuhumu,* small trigger fish
(from reduplication of Proto-Polynesian **sumu,* trigger fish)
+ *nukunuku,* small snout, reduplication of *nuku,* snout + *ā,*
like + *pua'a,* pig.]

i·con·o·clast (ī-kŏn′ə-klăst′)

noun

1. One who attacks and seeks to overthrow traditional or popular ideas or institutions: *"I think that nobody but a damned iconoclast could even conceive the atrocity you're proposing. I think you're one of those people who take pleasure in smashing apart anything that's stamped with tradition or stability"* (Stanley Ellin, "The Moment of Decision"). **2.** One who destroys sacred religious images.

[French *iconoclaste,* from Medieval Greek *eikonoklastēs,*
smasher of religious images : *eikono-,* image + Greek *-klastēs,*
breaker (from Greek *klān, klas-,* to break).]

₰ *Eikonoklastēs*, the ancestor of our word *iconoclast*, was first formed in Medieval Greek from the elements *eikōn*, "image, likeness," and *-klastēs*, "breaker," from *klān*, "to break." The images referred to by the word are religious images, which were the subject of controversy among Christians of the Byzantine Empire in the eighth and ninth centuries, when iconoclasm was at its height. In addition to destroying many sculptures and paintings, those opposed to images attempted to have them barred from display and veneration. During the Protestant Reformation, images in churches were again felt to be idolatrous and were once more banned and destroyed. *Iconoclast*, the descendant of the Greek word, is first recorded in English (1641), with reference to the Byzantine iconoclasts.

38

in·sou·ci·ant (ĭn-soō′sē-ənt)

adjective

Marked by blithe unconcern; nonchalant: *"No man, save the Texas Ranger, has ever carried it [the revolver] with the insouciant air and picturesque charm of the American cowboy"* (Ramon F. Adams, *Cowboy Lingo*).

[French : *in-*, not + *souciant*, present participle of *soucier*, to trouble (from Old French, from Vulgar Latin **sollicītāre*, alteration of Latin *sollicitāre*, to vex).]

in·ter·lop·er (ĭn′tər-lō′pər)

noun

1. One that interferes with the affairs of others, often for selfish reasons; a meddler: *"The Alexandria of my childhood was still a pure Southern culture, undiluted yet by suburban interlopers from up north"* (James Carroll, *An American Requiem*). **2.** One that intrudes in a place, situation, or activity. **3.** *Archaic* **a.** One that trespasses on a trade monopoly, as by conducting unauthorized trade in an area designated to a chartered company. **b.** A ship or other vessel used in such trade.

[From English *inter-* (from Latin, between) + probably Middle Dutch *lōper,* runner (from *lōpen,* to run).]

⊱ The word *interloper* first appeared as England embarked on the course that led to the British Empire. First recorded around 1590 in connection with the Muscovy Company, the earliest major English trading company (chartered in 1555), *interloper* was soon used in connection with independent traders competing with the East India Company (chartered in 1600) as well. These monopolies held a dim view of independent traders, called *interlopers.* The term is probably partly derived from Dutch, the language of one of the great trade rivals of the English at that time. *Inter-* is simply the prefix *inter-,* meaning "between, among." The element *-loper* is probably related to the same element in *landloper,* "vagabond," a word adopted from Middle Dutch, where it is a compound of *land,* "land," and *lōper* (from *lōpen,* "to run, leap"). *Interloper* came to be used in the extended sense "busybody" in the 1600s.

in·ter·nec·ine

(ĭn′tər-nĕs′ēn′, ĭn′tər-nĕs′ĭn, ĭn′tər-nē′sīn′)

adjective

1. Of or relating to struggle within a nation, organization, or group: *"While he was becoming more and more closely drawn into the internecine politics of the Socialist party and its pro-Bolshevik and anti-Bolshevik offshoots, she was getting a broader sense of the country, of what the Russian experiment meant to various people"* (Mary V. Dearborn, *Queen of Bohemia*). **2.** Mutually destructive; ruinous or fatal to both sides. **3.** Characterized by bloodshed or carnage.

[Latin *internecīnus,* destructive, variant of *internecīvus,* from *internecāre,* to slaughter : *inter-,* intensive prefix + *nex, nec-,* death.]

🐾 Today, *internecine* usually means "relating to internal struggle," but in its first recorded use in English, in 1663, it meant "fought to the death," as did the Latin source of the word, derived from the verb *necāre,* "to kill." Here, the prefix *inter-* did not have the usual sense of "between, mutual" but rather that of an intensifier meaning "all the way, to the death." Samuel Johnson was unaware of this fact when he compiled his great dictionary in the 1700s. Misunderstanding the prefix, he defined *internecine* as "endeavoring mutual destruction." Johnson's dictionary was so popular and considered so authoritative that this error became widely adopted. It was further compounded when *internecine* acquired the sense "relating to internal struggle." Since the ultimate arbiter of language is how people use it, what was once a compounded error has long since become an acceptable usage.

in·vei·gle (ĭn-vā′gəl, ĭn-vē′gəl)

transitive verb
> Past participle and past tense: **in·vei·gled**
> Present participle: **in·vei·gling**
> Third person singular present tense: **in·vei·gles**

1. To win over by coaxing, flattery, or artful talk: *"Melmotte is, in short, a mighty con artist: we are on to him almost instantly. Our interest is not in finding out his scam, but in watching him inveigle and enmesh the gullible"* (Cynthia Ozick, *The New York Times Book Review*). **2.** To obtain by cajolery.

[Middle English *envegle,* alteration of Old French *aveugler,* to blind, from *aveugle,* blind, from Vulgar Latin **aboculus* : Latin *ab-,* away from + Latin *oculus,* eye (probably loan-translation of Gaulish *exsops* : *exs-,* from + *ops,* eye).]

jer·e·mi·ad (jĕr′ə-mī′əd)

noun

A literary work or speech expressing a bitter lament or a righteous prophecy of doom.

[French *jérémiade,* after *Jérémie,* Jeremiah, prophet to whom the biblical book of Lamentations is traditionally attributed, from Late Latin *Ieremiās,* from Hebrew *yirməyāhû,* Yahweh has established : *yirm,* he has established + *yāhû,* Yahweh.]

43
jux·ta·po·si·tion (jŭk′stə-pə-zĭsh′ən)

noun

The act or an instance of placing two items side by side, especially for comparison or contrast, or the state of being so placed: *"No human eye can isolate the unhappy coincidence of line and place which suggests evil in the face of a house, and yet somehow a maniac juxtaposition, a badly turned angle, some chance meeting of roof and sky, turned Hill House into a place of despair, more frightening because the face of Hill House seemed awake, with a watchfulness from the blank windows and a touch of glee in the eyebrow of a cornice"* (Shirley Jackson, *The Haunting of Hill House*).

[French *juxtaposition* : Latin *iūxtā*, close by + French *position*, position, from Latin *positiō, positiōn-*, placing, position, from *positus*, past participle of *pōnere*, to place.]

44
ko·an (kō′än′)

noun

A puzzling, often paradoxical statement or story, used in Zen Buddhism as an aid to meditation and a means of gaining spiritual awakening: *"Saskia will sit for an hour in the grass down by the shore, pondering a koan until she enters that space wherein silence and stillness press against her like solid walls"* (Brian Hall, *The Saskiad*).

[Japanese *kōan* : *kō*, public + *an*, matter for consideration, legal case.]

They were not welcomed home very cordially by their mother. Mrs. Bennet wondered at their coming, and thought them very wrong to give so much trouble, and was sure Jane would have caught cold again; but their father, though very **laconic** in his expressions of pleasure, was really glad to see them; he had felt their importance in the family circle.

— Jane Austen,
Pride and Prejudice

45
la·con·ic (lə-kŏn′ĭk)

adjective

Using few words; terse; concise: *"[T]heir father, though very laconic in his expressions of pleasure, was really glad to see them"* (Jane Austen, *Pride and Prejudice*).

[Latin *Lacōnicus*, Spartan, from Greek *Lakōnikos*, from *Lakōn*, a Spartan (from the reputation of the Spartans for brevity of speech).]

The study of the classics allows us to understand the history of the term *laconic*, which comes to English via Latin from Greek *Lakōnikos*. The English word is first recorded in 1583 with the sense "of or relating to Laconia or its inhabitants." *Lakōnikos* is derived from *Lakōn*, "a Laconian, a person from Lacedaemon," the name for the region of Greece of which Sparta was the capital. The Spartans, noted for being warlike and disciplined, were also known for the brevity of their speech, and it is this quality that English writers still denote by the use of the adjective *laconic*, which is first found in this sense in 1589.

46
la·gniappe (lăn′yəp, lăn-yăp′)

noun
Chiefly southern Louisiana and Mississippi

1. A small gift presented by a storeowner to a customer with the customer's purchase. **2.** An extra or unexpected gift or benefit.

[Louisiana French, from American Spanish *la ñapa,* the gift : *la,* the + *ñapa* (variant of *yapa,* gift, from Quechua, from *yapay,* to give more).]

🏵️ *Lagniappe* derives from New World Spanish *la ñapa,* "the gift," and ultimately from Quechua *yapay,* "to give more." The word entered the rich Creole dialect mixture of New Orleans and there acquired a French spelling. It is still used in the Gulf states, especially southern Louisiana, to denote a little bonus that a friendly shopkeeper might add to a purchase. By extension, it may mean "an extra or unexpected gift or benefit."

47
lep·re·chaun (lĕp′rĭ-kŏn′, lĕp′rĭ-kôn′)

noun

One of a race of elves in Irish folklore who can reveal hidden treasure to those who catch them.

[Irish Gaelic *luprachán,* alteration of Middle Irish *luchrupán,* from Old Irish *luchorpán : luchorp* (*lú*-, small + *corp,* body, from *Latin* corpus) + *-án,* diminutive suffix.]

🏵️ Nothing seems more Irish than the leprechaun, yet hiding within the word *leprechaun* is a word from another language entirely. *Leprechaun* ultimately derives from Old Irish *luchorpán,* a compound of Old Irish *lú,* meaning "small," and the Old Irish word *corp,* "body." *Corp* is borrowed from Latin *corpus* (which can be seen in such words as *corporal,* "physical; relating to the

---

body"). This fact is a piece of evidence attesting to the influence of Latin on the Irish language. Although *leprechaun* is old in Irish, it is fairly new in English, being first recorded in 1604.

48 li·to·tes (lī′tə-tēz′, lĭt′ə-tēz′, lī-tō′tēz)

noun
> Plural: **litotes**

A figure of speech consisting of an understatement in which an affirmative is expressed by negating its opposite, as in *"I showed him over the establishment, not omitting the pantry, with <u>no little</u> pride, and he commended it highly"* (Charles Dickens, *David Copperfield*).

[Greek *lītotēs,* from *lītos,* plain.]

49 lu·cu·brate (lōō′kyŏŏ-brāt′)

intransitive verb
> Past participle and past tense: **lu·cu·brat·ed**
> Present participle: **lu·cu·brat·ing**
> Third person singular present tense: **lu·cu·brates**

To write in a scholarly fashion; produce scholarship.

[Latin *lūcubrāre,* to work at night by lamplight.]

50

mag·nan·i·mous (măg-năn′ə-məs)

adjective

Noble in mind and heart; generous and unselfish: *"[S]ophisticated and intellectually wise as I like to think I am now, I have to admit I'm still inspired by a poetic phrase, a magnanimous gesture, a promise of a better tomorrow"* (Norma Sherry, *Baltimore Chronicle & Sentinel*).

[From Latin *magnanimus* : *magnus*, great + *animus*, soul, mind.]

51

ma·ha·ra·jah *or* **ma·ha·ra·ja**
(mä′hə-rä′jə, mä′hə-rä′zhə)

noun

1. A king or prince in India ranking above a rajah, especially the sovereign of one of the former native states. **2.** Used as a title for such a king or prince.

[Sanskrit *mahārājaḥ* : *mahā-*, great + *rājā, rājaḥ*, king.]

ℬ *Maharajah* comes from the Sanskrit word *mahārājaḥ*, meaning "great king." The element *mahā-* is related to Greek *mega-* and Latin *magnus*, both meaning the same thing as the Sanskrit term, "great." All three forms derive from an Indo-European root that also has descendants in Germanic, in particular, the Old English word *micel*, pronounced (mĭ′chəl). This survives today in *much* (shortened from Middle English *muchel*).

mal·a·prop·ism (măl′ə-prŏp-ĭz′əm)

noun

1. Ludicrous misuse of a word, especially by confusion with one of similar sound. **2.** An example of such misuse.

[After Mrs. Malaprop (from *malapropos*), a character in *The Rivals*, a play by Richard Brinsley Sheridan + *-ism*, nominal suffix.]

"She's as headstrong as an allegory on the banks of the Nile" and "He is the very pineapple of politeness" are two of the absurd pronouncements from Mrs. Malaprop that explain why her name became synonymous with ludicrous misuse of language. A character in Richard Brinsley Sheridan's play *The Rivals* (1775), Mrs. Malaprop consistently uses language malapropos, that is, inappropriately. The word *malapropos* comes from the French phrase *mal à propos*, made up of *mal*, "badly," *à*, "to," and *propos*, "purpose, subject," and means "inappropriate." *The Rivals* was a popular play, and Mrs. Malaprop became enshrined in a common noun, first in the form *malaprop* and later in *malapropism*, which is first recorded in 1830. Perhaps that is what Mrs. Malaprop feared when she said, "If I reprehend any thing in this world, it is the use of my oracular tongue, and a nice derangement of epitaphs!"

mer·e·tri·cious (mĕr′ĭ-trĭsh′əs)

adjective

1a. Attracting attention in a vulgar manner: *"It was a platinum fob chain simple and chaste in design, properly proclaiming its value by substance alone and not by meretricious ornamentation—as all good things should do"* (O. Henry, "The Gift of the Magi"). **b.** Plausible but false or insincere; specious: *I saw through his meretricious arguments.* **2.** Of or relating to prostitutes or prostitution.

[Latin *meretrīcius,* of prostitutes, from *meretrīx, meretrīc-,* prostitute, from *merēre,* to earn money.]

54

mes·mer·ize (mĕz′mə-rīz′, mĕs′mə-rīz′)

transitive verb

Past participle and past tense: **mes·mer·ized**
Present participle: **mes·mer·iz·ing**
Third person singular present tense: **mes·mer·iz·es**

1. To spellbind; enthrall: "*He could mesmerize an audience by the sheer force of his presence*" (Justin Kaplan). "*The other morning I watched five game shows in a row on television. I wanted to turn them off, but I was too mesmerized by the contestants*" (Erma Bombeck, *If Life Is a Bowl of Cherries, What Am I Doing in the Pits?*). **2.** To hypnotize.

[After Franz Mesmer (1734–1815), Austrian physician.]

Franz Anton Mesmer, a visionary eighteenth-century physician, believed cures could be effected by having patients do things such as sit with their feet in a fountain of magnetized water while holding cables attached to magnetized trees. He then came to believe that magnetic powers resided in himself, and during highly fashionable curative sessions in Paris he caused his patients to have reactions ranging from sleeping or dancing to convulsions. These reactions were actually brought about by hypnotic powers that Mesmer was unaware he possessed. One of his pupils, named Puységur, then used the term *mesmerism* (first recorded in English in 1802) for Mesmer's practices. The related word *mesmerize* (first recorded in English in 1829), having shed its reference to the hypnotic doctor, lives on in the sense "to enthrall."

me·tic·u·lous (mĭ-tĭk′yə-ləs)

adjective

1. Extremely careful and precise: *"[H]is wardrobe seemed to consist entirely of meticulous reconstructions of garments of the previous century"* (William Gibson, *Neuromancer*). **2.** Extremely or excessively concerned with details.

[From Latin *metīculōsus*, timid, from *metus*, fear.]

Case had never seen him wear the same suit twice, although his wardrobe seemed to consist entirely of **meticulous** reconstructions of garments of the previous century. He affected prescription lenses, framed in spidery gold, ground from pink slabs of synthetic quartz and beveled like the mirrors in a Victorian dollhouse.

—William Gibson,
Neuromancer

mi·lieu (mĭl-yŏŏ′, mĭ-lyœ′)

noun
> Plural: **mi·lieus** *or* **mi·lieux** (mĭ-lyœ′)

An environment or a setting: *"I don't know that the arts have a milieu here, any of them; they're more like a very thinly settled outskirt"* (Edith Wharton, *The Age of Innocence*).

[French, from Old French, center : *mi,* middle (from Latin *medius*) + *lieu,* place (from Latin *locus*).]

mi·to·chon·dri·on (mī′tə-kŏn′drē-ən)

noun
> Plural **mi·to·chon·dri·a** (mī′tə-kŏn′drē-ə)

A structure that is found in the cytoplasm of all cells except bacteria; has an inner membrane enclosing a liquid that contains DNA (genetically different from nuclear DNA), RNA, small ribosomes, and solutes; and breaks down food molecules and converts them to usable energy in the presence of oxygen.

[New Latin : Greek *mitos,* warp thread + Greek *khondrion,* diminutive of *khondros,* grain, granule.]

nem·e·sis (nĕm′ĭ-sĭs)

noun

Plural: **nem·e·ses** (nĕm′ĭ-sēz′)

1. A source of harm or ruin: *"The resolutions—calling for limitations on working hours, state support for education, nationalization of railways—were not very revolutionary. Reform was again showing itself to be the nemesis of revolution"* (John Kenneth Galbraith, *The Age of Uncertainty*). **2.** Retributive justice in its execution or outcome. **3.** An opponent that cannot be beaten or overcome. **4.** One that inflicts retribution or vengeance. **5. Nemesis** In Greek mythology, the goddess of retributive justice or vengeance.

[Greek, retribution, the goddess Nemesis, from *nemein,* to allot.]

59

nic·ti·tate (nĭk′tĭ-tāt′) *also* **nic·tate** (nĭk′tāt′)

intransitive verb
    Past participle and past tense: **nic·ti·tat·ed**
    Present participle: **nic·ti·tat·ing**
    Third person singular present tense: **nic·ti·tates**

To wink. Used especially in connection with the *nicti-tating membrane,* a transparent inner eyelid in birds, reptiles, and some mammals that closes to protect and moisten the eye.

[Medieval Latin *nictitāre,* frequentative of Latin *nictāre,* to wink.]

nos·trum (nŏs**′**trəm)

noun

1. A medicine whose effectiveness is unproved and whose ingredients are usually secret; a quack remedy: *"He was clearly a confirmed hypochondriac, and I was dreamily conscious that he was pouring forth interminable trains of symptoms, and imploring information as to the composition and action of innumerable quack nostrums, some of which he bore about in a leather case in his pocket"* (Arthur Conan Doyle, *The Sign of Four*). **2.** A favored but often questionable remedy: *"His economic nostrums of lowering taxes to feed the economy were the subject of furious debates"* (David Shribman, *Boston Globe*).

[From Latin *nostrum (remedium)*, our (remedy), neuter of *noster*.]

nud·nik *also* **nud·nick** (nŏŏd**′**nĭk)

noun

Slang An obtuse, boring, or bothersome person; a pest.

[Yiddish, from *nudne*, boring, from *nudyen*, to bore + *-nik*, -nik, nominal suffix.]

I find that all the fair and noble impulses of humanity, the dreams of poets and the agonies of martyrs, are shackled and bound in the service of organized and predatory Greed! And therefore I cannot rest, I cannot be silent; therefore I cast aside comfort and happiness, health and good repute — and go out into the world and cry out the pain of my spirit! Therefore I am not to be silenced by poverty and sickness, not by hatred and **obloquy,** by threats and ridicule — not by prison and persecution, if they should come — not by any power that is upon the earth or above the earth, that was, or is, or ever can be created.

— Upton Sinclair,
The Jungle

ob·lo·quy (ŏb′lə-kwē)

noun
Plural: **ob·lo·quies**

1. Abusively detractive language or utterance; calumny: *"Therefore I am not to be silenced by poverty and sickness, not by hatred and obloquy, by threats and ridicule"* (Upton Sinclair, *The Jungle*). **2.** The condition of disgrace suffered as a result of abuse or vilification; ill repute.

[Middle English *obloqui*, from Late Latin *obloquium*, abusive contradiction, from Latin *obloquī*, to interrupt : *ob-*, against + *loquī*, to speak.]

ob·strep·er·ous (ŏb-strĕp′ər-əs)

adjective

Noisily unruly or defiant: *"Nurse Hopkins ran the day-care center on the top floor of the agency building, and if from time to time she used tranquilizers on the more obstreperous children, she was at least trained and qualified to do so, and she knew what side effects to look out for"* (Faye Weldon, *The Life and Loves of a She-Devil*).

[From Latin *obstreperus*, noisy, from *obstrepere*, to make a noise against : *ob-*, against + *strepere*, to make a noise (of imitative origin).]

64

ox·y·mo·ron (ŏk′sē-môr′ŏn′)

noun

Plural: **ox·y·mo·rons**
or **ox·y·mo·ra** (ŏk′sē-môr′ə)

A rhetorical figure in which incongruous or contradictory terms are combined, as in *deafening silence.*

[Greek *oxumōron,* from neuter of *oxumōros,* pointedly foolish : *oxus,* sharp, + *mōros,* foolish, dull.]

⅋ Interestingly, the word *oxymoron* is itself etymologically an oxymoron. Combined, the Greek words *oxus* and *mōros,* which mean respectively "sharp" and "dull," form the compound *oxumōros,* "pointedly foolish."

65

pa·lav·er (pə-lăv′ər, pə-lä′vər)

noun

1a. Idle chatter. **b.** Talk intended to charm or beguile: *"The girl glanced back at him over her shoulder and said with great bitterness: –The men that is now is only all palaver and what they can get out of you"* (James Joyce, "The Dead," *Dubliners*). **2.** A parley between two groups, especially European explorers and representatives of local populations.

[Portuguese *palavra,* speech, alteration of Late Latin *parabola,* speech, parable.]

—O, then, said Gabriel gaily, I suppose we'll be going to your wedding one of these fine days with your young man, eh?

The girl glanced back at him over her shoulder and said with great bitterness:

—The men that is now is only all **palaver** and what they can get out of you.

— James Joyce,
"The Dead," *Dubliners*

pe·jor·a·tive

(pĭ-jôr′ə-tĭv, pĕj′ə-rā′tĭv, pē′jə-rā′tĭv)

adjective

Disparaging; belittling: "*Unfortunately, the word 'diet' has come to have a pejorative meaning for many people because it suggests denial, restriction, or limitations*" (James E. Marti, *The Ultimate Consumer's Guide to Diets and Nutrition*).

noun

A disparaging or belittling word or expression.

[From *pejorate,* to make worse (from Late Latin *pēiōrātus,* past participle of *pēiōrāre,* to make worse, from Latin *pēior,* worse), + *-ive,* adjectival suffix (from Latin *-īvus*).]

pre·car·i·ous (prĭ-kâr′ē-əs)

adjective

1. Dangerously lacking in security or stability: "*And the recurring sight of hitch-hikers waiting against the sky gave him the flash of a sensation he had known as a child: standing still with nothing to touch him, feeling tall and having the world come all at once into its round shape underfoot and rush and turn through space and make his stand very precarious and lonely*" (Eudora Welty, "The Hitch-Hikers"). **2.** Subject to chance or uncertain conditions: *The people eked out a precarious existence in the mountains.* **3.** Based on uncertain, unwarranted, or unproved premises: *a precarious solution to a difficult problem.*

[From Latin *precārius,* obtained by entreaty, uncertain, from *precārī,* to entreat.]

68

pres·ti·dig·i·ta·tion (prĕs′tĭ-dĭj′ĭ-tā′shən)

noun

1. Performance of or skill in performing magic or con-
juring tricks with the hands; sleight of hand. **2.** Skill or
cleverness, especially in deceiving others.

[French (influenced by *prestigiateur*, juggler, conjurer, from
prestige, illusion), from *prestidigitateur*, conjurer : *preste*,
nimble (from Italian *presto*) + Latin *digitus*, finger.]

69

pre·ter·nat·u·ral
(prē′tər-năch′ər-əl, prē′tər-năch′rəl)

adjective

1. Differing from what is normal or natural; abnor-
mal or extraordinary: *"Dickens, with preternatural ap-
prehension of the language of manners, and the varieties
of street life, with pathos and laughter, with patriotic and
still enlarging generosity, writes London tracts"* (Ralph
Waldo Emerson, *English Traits*). **2.** Transcending the
natural or material order; supernatural.

[Medieval Latin *praeternātūrālis*, from Latin *praeter
nātūrām*, beyond nature : *praeter*, beyond + *nātūra*, nature.]

quark (kwôrk, kwärk)

noun

Any of a group of elementary particles supposed to be the fundamental units that combine to make up the subatomic particles known as hadrons (baryons, such as neutrons and protons, and mesons). Quarks have fractional electric charges, such as one-third the charge of an electron.

[From "Three quarks for Muster Mark!," a line in *Finnegans Wake* by James Joyce.]

𝄢 "Three quarks for Muster Mark!/Sure he hasn't got much of a bark/And sure any he has it's all beside the mark." This passage from James Joyce's *Finnegans Wake,* part of a poem directed against King Mark, the cuckolded husband in the Tristan legend, has left its mark on modern physics. Packed with names of birds and words suggestive of birds, the poem and accompanying prose are a squawk against the king that suggests the cawing of a crow. The word *quark* comes from the standard English verb *quark,* meaning "to caw, croak," and also from the dialectal verb *quawk,* meaning "to caw, screech like a bird." But why should *quark* have become the name for a group of hypothetical subatomic particles proposed as the fundamental units of matter? Murray Gell-Mann, the physicist who proposed this name for these particles, said in a private letter of June 27, 1978, to the editor of the *Oxford English Dictionary* that he had been influenced by Joyce's words: "The allusion to three quarks seemed perfect" (originally there were only three subatomic quarks). Gell-Mann, however, wanted to pronounce the word with (ô), not (ä), as Joyce seemed to indicate by rhymes such as *Mark*. Gell-Mann got around that "by supposing that one ingredient of the line 'Three quarks for Muster Mark' was a cry of 'Three quarts for Mister . . .' heard in H.C. Earwicker's pub," a plausible suggestion given the complex punning in Joyce's novel. It seems appropriate that this perplexing and humorous novel should have supplied the term for particles that come in six "flavors" and three "colors."

71

quix·ot·ic (kwĭk-sŏt/ĭk)

adjective

Caught up in the pursuit of unreachable goals; foolishly idealistic and impractical: *"[W]hat I like best in you is this particular enthusiasm, which is not at all practical or sensible, which is downright Quixotic"* (Willa Cather, *The Song of the Lark*).

[After Don Quixote, hero of a novel by Miguel de Cervantes Saavedra (1547–1616).]

72

red·o·lent (rĕd′l-ənt)

adjective

1. Fragrant; aromatic. **2.** Suggestive; reminiscent: *"There was a ripe mystery about it, a hint . . . of romances that were not musty and laid away already in lavender, but fresh and breathing and redolent of this year's shining motor-cars and of dances whose flowers were scarcely withered"* (F. Scott Fitzgerald, *The Great Gatsby*).

[Middle English, from Old French, from Latin *redolēns, redolent-,* present participle of *redolēre,* to smell : *re-, red-,* re-, intensive prefix + *olēre,* to smell.]

It amazed him — he had never been in such a beautiful house before. But what gave it an air of breathless intensity was that Daisy lived there — it was as casual a thing to her as his tent out at camp was to him. There was a ripe mystery about it, a hint of bedrooms upstairs more beautiful and cool than other bedrooms, of gay and radiant activities taking place through its corridors, and of romances that were not musty and laid away already in lavender, but fresh and breathing and **redolent** of this year's shining motor-cars and of dances whose flowers were scarcely withered.

— F. Scott Fitzgerald,
The Great Gatsby

re·pug·nant (rĭ-pŭg'nənt)

adjective

Arousing disgust or aversion; offensive or repulsive: "*There was her milk, untouched, forgotten, barely tepid. She drank it down, without pleasure; all its whiteness, draining from the stringing wet whiteness of the empty cup, was singularly repugnant*" (James Agee, *A Death in the Family*).

[Middle English, antagonistic, from Old French, from Latin *repugnāns, repugnant-,* present participle of *repugnāre,* to fight against : *re-, red-,* against + *pugnāre,* to fight, from *pugnus,* fist.]

ru·bric (roo'brĭk)

noun

1. A class or category: "*This mission is sometimes discussed under the rubric of 'horizontal escalation' . . . from conventional to nuclear war*" (Jack Beatty, *Atlantic Monthly*). **2.** A part of a manuscript or book, such as a title, heading, or initial letter, that appears in decorative red lettering or is otherwise distinguished from the rest of the text. **3.** A title or heading in a code of law. **4.** A direction in a missal, hymnal, or other liturgical book: "*This kind of answer given in a measured official tone, as of a clergyman reading according to the rubric, did not help to . . . justify the glories of the Eternal City, or to give her the hope that if she knew more about them the world would be joyously illuminated for her*" (George Eliot, *Middlemarch*). **5.** An authoritative rule or direction: "*The creative ferment of the Internet . . . is frequently in-*

voked by the legislative legions in Washington who want to extend some version of electronic networking to every home, school, library and hospital in the country under the rubric of a National Information Infrastructure" (Gary Stix, *Scientific American*). **6.** A form of hematite used as a red pigment.

adjective

1. Red or reddish. **2.** Written in red.

[Middle English *rubrike*, heading, title, from Old French *rubrique*, from Latin *rubrīca*, red chalk, from *ruber, rubr-*, red.]

sang-froid *or* **sang·froid** (säN-frwä′)

noun

Coolness and composure, especially in trying circumstances: *"For a moment his face became a white mask of horror, but he soon recovered his sang-froid and, looking up at Lady Windermere, said with a forced smile, 'It is the hand of a charming young man'"* (Oscar Wilde, *Lord Arthur Savile's Crime*).

[French : *sang*, blood (from Old French, from Latin *sanguis*) + *froid*, cold (from Old French, from Vulgar Latin **frigidus*, alteration of Latin *frīgidus*).]

sar·coph·a·gus (sär-kŏf′ə-gəs)

noun

> Plural: **sar·coph·a·gi** *or* **sar·coph·a·gus·es**
> (sär-kŏf′ə-jī′)

A stone coffin, often inscribed or decorated with sculpture.

[Latin, from Greek *sarkophagos,* coffin, from *(lithos) sarkophagos,* limestone that consumed the flesh of corpses laid in it : *sarx, sark-,* flesh + *-phagos,* eating, feeding on.]

The macabre word *sarcophagus* comes to us from Latin and Greek, having been derived in Greek from *sarx,* "flesh," and *phagein,* "to eat." The Greek word *sarkophagos* meant "eating flesh," and in the phrase *lithos* ("stone") *sarkophagos,* it denoted a limestone that was thought to decompose the flesh of corpses placed in it. Used by itself as a noun the Greek term came to mean "coffin." The term was carried over into Latin, where *sarcophagus* was used in the phrase *lapis* ("stone") *sarcophagus,* referring to the same stone as in Greek. *Sarcophagus* used as a noun in Latin meant "coffin of any material." This Latin word was borrowed into English, first being recorded in 1601 with reference to the flesh-consuming stone and then in 1705 with reference to a stone coffin.

schwa (shwä)

noun

1. A vowel that is articulated with the tongue in the middle of the oral cavity, typically occurring in unstressed syllables as the first vowel of *about* or the final vowel of *sofa.* **2.** The symbol (ə) used to represent this

---

sound. In some phonetic systems it also represents the sounds of such vowels in stressed positions, as in *but*.

[German, from Hebrew, *šəwā'*, probably from Syriac *(nuqzē) šwayyā*, even (points), plural passive participle of *šwā*, to be even.]

78

ser·en·dip·i·ty (sĕr'ən-dĭp'ĭ-tē)

noun
Plural: **ser·en·dip·i·ties**

1. The faculty of making fortunate discoveries by accident. **2.** The fact or occurrence of such discoveries. **3.** An instance of making such a discovery.

[From the characters in the Persian fairy tale *The Three Princes of Serendip*, who made such discoveries, from Persian *Sarandīp*, Sri Lanka, from Arabic *Sarandīb*.]

℘ We are indebted to the English author Horace Walpole for the word *serendipity*, which he coined in one of the 3,000 or more letters that make up an important part of his literary legacy. In a letter of January 28, 1754, Walpole says that "this discovery, indeed, is almost of that kind which I call Serendipity, a very expressive word." Walpole formed the word on an old name for Sri Lanka, *Serendip*. He explained that this name was part of the title of "a silly fairy tale, called *The Three Princes of Serendip*: as their highnesses traveled, they were always making discoveries, by accidents and sagacity, of things which they were not in quest of. . . ."

---

ses·qui·pe·da·lian (sĕs′kwĭ-pĭ-dāl′yən)

adjective

1. Given to or characterized by the use of long words.
2. Having many syllables; polysyllabic: *"[R]ecently a strange whimsy has started to creep in among the sesquipedalian prose of scientific journals"* (Stephen S. Hall, *The New York Times*).

noun

A long word.

[From Latin *sēsquipedālis*, of a foot and a half in length : *sēsqui-, sesqui-* + *pēs, ped-*, foot + *-ian*, nominal and adjectival suffix.]

sha·man (shä′mən, shā′mən)

noun
  Plural: **sha·mans**

A member of certain tribal societies who acts as a medium between the visible world and an invisible spirit world and practices magic or sorcery for healing, divination, and control over natural events.

[Russian, from Evenki *šaman*, Buddhist monk, shaman, from Tocharian B *ṣamāne*, monk, from Prakrit *ṣamana*, from Sanskrit *śramaṇaḥ*, from *śrámaḥ*, religious exercise.]

꧁ At first glance, *shaman* may seem to be a compound of *-man* and a mysterious prefix *sha-*. In fact, its far different and more remarkable history begins in India as the Sanskrit word *śramaṇaḥ*, "ascetic, Buddhist monk." In the Prakrit languages, which descended from Sanskrit, it developed into *ṣamana*, a term that spread with Buddhism over central Asia. It was borrowed into Tocharian B and probably from there into Evenki (a Tungusic language of Siberian reindeer herders), where the word referred to a healer or a person who communicated with the spirit world. The term was then borrowed into Russian and other European languages and then into English.

Shaman is probably the only English word that has come from or passed through a Tocharian language. The two closely related Tocharian languages, Tocharian A and Tocharian B, are now extinct. The Tocharians lived along the Silk Road in the eastern Turkistan (Xinjiang Uygur Autonomous Region in China). We know their languages from documents such as travelers' caravan passes and Buddhist sutras written around 600–800 AD. Together, Tocharian A and B constitute a separate branch of the family tree of the Indo-European languages, the family to which English also belongs.

81

si·ne·cure (sī′nĭ-kyŏŏr′, sĭn′ĭ-kyŏŏr′)

noun

1. A position or office that requires little or no work but provides a salary: *"Be it said, that in this vocation of whaling, sinecures are unknown; dignity and danger go hand in hand; till you get to be Captain, the higher you rise the harder you toil"* (Herman Melville, *Moby-Dick*).
2. *Archaic* An ecclesiastical benefice not attached to the spiritual duties of a parish.

[From Medieval Latin *(beneficium) sine cūrā*, (benefice) without spiritual care (of souls).]

82

snake·bit (snāk′bĭt′)
   also **snake·bit·ten** (snāk′bĭt′n)

adjective

Experiencing a period of misfortune or inability to suc-
ceed; unlucky: *Having lost four games in a row by one
run, the pitcher was starting to feel a little snakebit.*

83

sop·o·rif·ic (sŏp′ə-rĭf′ĭk)

adjective

1. Inducing or tending to induce sleep: "*[T]he heavy
supper she had eaten produced a soporific effect: she was
already snoring before I had finished undressing*" (Charlotte Brontë, *Jane Eyre*). **2.** Drowsy.

noun

A drug or other substance that induces sleep; a hypnotic.

[From *sopor-*, sleep (from Latin *sopor*) + *-fic, -ific,* causing,
making (from Latin *-ficus,* from *facere,* to make, do).]

I had to sit with the girls during their hour of study; then it was my turn to read prayers; to see them to bed: afterwards I supped with the other teachers. Even when we finally retired for the night, the inevitable Miss Gryce was still my companion: we had only a short end of candle in our candlestick, and I dreaded lest she should talk till it was all burnt out; fortunately, however, the heavy supper she had eaten produced a **soporific** effect: she was already snoring before I had finished undressing.

— Charlotte Brontë,
Jane Eyre

84
suc·co·tash (sŭk′ə-tăsh′)

noun

A stew consisting of kernels of corn, lima beans, and tomatoes.

[Narragansett *msíckquatash,* boiled whole-kernel corn.]

85
su·sur·ra·tion (soo′sə-rā′shən)

noun

A soft whispering or rustling sound; a murmur: *"The rain was now falling more steadily, with a low, monotonous susurration, interrupted at long intervals by the sudden slashing of the boughs of the trees as the wind rose and failed"* (Ambrose Bierce, *Can Such Things Be?*).

[Middle English *susurracioun,* from Late Latin *susurrātiō, susurrātiōn-,* from Latin *susurrātus,* past participle of *susurrāre,* to whisper, from *susurrus,* whisper, ultimately of imitative origin.]

86
syz·y·gy (sĭz′ə-jē′)

noun
  Plural: **syz·y·gies**

An alignment of three celestial bodies, especially the sun, the moon, and Earth, in which all three bodies lie along a single straight line: *After a solar eclipse, it is likely*

---

succotash / tantalize

*that there will be another eclipse somewhere on Earth at
the next syzygy.* **2.** The combining of two feet into a
single metrical unit in classical prosody.

[Late Latin *sȳzygia*, from Greek *suzugiā*, union, from *suzu-
gos*, paired : *sun-*, *su-*, with, together + *zugon*, yoke.]

87

tan·ta·lize (tăn′tə-līz′)

transitive verb
> Past participle and past tense: **tan·ta·lized**
> Present participle: **tan·ta·liz·ing**
> Third person singular present tense: **tan·ta·liz·es**

To excite (another) by exposing something desirable,
especially while keeping it out of reach: *"Finer than human hair, lighter than cotton, and—ounce for ounce—
stronger than steel, silk tantalizes materials researchers
seeking to duplicate its properties or synthesize it for large-
scale production"* (Richard Lipkin, *Science News*).

[From Latin *Tantalus*, Tantalus.]

꧁ *Tantalize* comes from *Tantalus*, the name of a mythical king of
Lydia, a territory on the Aegean Sea in the west of Asia Minor
(now Turkey). Tantalus, originally one of the luckiest of mortals, enjoyed the privilege of feasting with the gods, but he sub-
sequently violated their hospitality. Some say he stole the food
of the gods, the *nectar* and *ambrosia* that bestow eternal life, and
gave it to mortals. Others say that he killed his own son Pelops
and served him to the gods to test whether they could recognize
the forbidden meat. Accordingly, the gods condemned Tantalus
to suffer everlasting hunger and thirst. He stands in a pool of
water that recedes when he bends to drink, and the branches of
the trees above him move out of reach when he tries to pluck
their fruit, *tantalizing* him for all eternity.

the·o·ry (thē′ə-rē, thîr′ē)

noun

Plural: **the·o·ries**

1. A set of statements or principles devised to explain a group of facts or phenomena, especially one that has been repeatedly tested or is widely accepted and can be used to make predictions about natural phenomena. **2.** The branch of a science or art consisting of its explanatory statements, accepted principles, and methods of analysis, as opposed to practice: *He was a fine musician but had never studied theory.* **3.** A set of theorems that constitute a systematic view of a branch of mathematics. **4.** Abstract reasoning; speculation: *Her decision was based on experience rather than theory.* **5.** A belief or principle that guides action or assists comprehension or judgment: *The detectives staked out the house on the theory that criminals usually return to the scene of the crime.* **6.** An assumption based on limited information or knowledge; a conjecture.

[Late Latin *theōria,* from Greek *theōriā,* from *theōros,* spectator : probably *theā,* a viewing + *-oros,* seeing (from *horān,* to see).]

❦ *Hypothesis, law,* and *theory* refer to different kinds of statements, or sets of statements, that scientists make about natural phenomena. A *hypothesis* is a proposition that attempts to explain a set of facts in a unified way. It generally forms the basis of experiments designed to establish its plausibility. Though a hypothesis can never be proven true (in fact, hypotheses generally leave some facts unexplained), it can sometimes be verified beyond reasonable doubt in the context of a particular theoretical approach. A scientific *law* is a hypothesis that is assumed to be universally true. A law has good predictive power, allowing a scientist to model a physical system and predict what will happen under various conditions. A *theory* is a set of statements, including laws and hypotheses, that explains a group of observations or phenomena in terms of those laws and hypotheses. A theory thus accounts for a wider variety of events than a law does. Broad acceptance of a theory comes when it has been tested repeatedly on new data and been used to make accurate predictions. Although a theory generally contains hypotheses that are still open to revision, sometimes it is hard to know where the hypothesis ends and the law or theory begins. Albert Einstein's theory of relativity, for example, consists of statements that were originally considered to be hypotheses (and daring at that). But all the hypotheses of relativity have now achieved the authority of scientific laws, and Einstein's theory has supplanted Newton's laws of motion. In some cases, such as the germ theory of infectious disease, a theory becomes so completely accepted, it stops being referred to as a theory.

89

tim·bre (tăm′bər, tĭm′bər)

noun

The combination of qualities of a sound that distinguishes it from other sounds of the same pitch and volume: *"John stared at Elisha all during the lesson, admiring the timbre of Elisha's voice, much deeper and manlier than his own"* (James Baldwin, *Go Tell It on the Mountain*).

[French, from Old French, drum, clapperless bell, probably from Medieval Greek *timbanon, drum, from earlier Greek tumpanon, kettledrum.]

He was not much older than John, only seventeen, and he was already saved and was a preacher. John stared at Elisha all during the lesson, admiring the **timbre** of Elisha's voice, much deeper and manlier than his own, admiring the leanness, and grace, and strength, and darkness of Elisha in his Sunday suit, wondering if he would ever be holy as Elisha was holy.

—James Baldwin,
Go Tell It on the Mountain

trog·lo·dyte (trŏg**′**lə-dīt**′**)

noun

1a. A member of a fabulous or prehistoric race of people that lived in caves, dens, or holes: *"Awkward, red-faced, too big for his shrinking suit and towering over the room like some club-wielding troglodyte, O'Kane could only duck his head and mumble an apology"* (T. Coraghessan Boyle, *Riven Rock*). **b.** A person considered to be reclusive, reactionary, out of date, or brutish. **2a.** An anthropoid ape, such as a gorilla. **b.** An animal that lives underground.

[From Latin *Trōglodytae,* a people said to be cave dwellers, from Greek *Trōglodutai,* alteration (influenced by *trōglē,* hole, and *-dutai,* those who enter), of *Trōgodutai.*]

ul·lage (ŭl**′**ĭj)

noun

1. The amount of liquid within a container that is lost, as by leakage, during shipment or storage. **2.** The amount by which a container, such as a bottle, cask, or tank, falls short of being full: *The ullage allows wine to expand in response to changes in temperature without pushing the cork out or bursting the bottle.*

[From Middle English *ulage,* from Old French *ouillage,* from *ouiller,* to fill up a cask, from *ouil,* eye, bunghole, from Latin *oculus,* eye.]

um·laut (o͞om′lout′)

noun

1a. A change in a vowel sound caused by partial assimilation especially to a vowel or semivowel in the following syllable. **b.** A vowel sound changed in this manner. **2.** The diacritic mark (¨) over a vowel, indicating an umlaut, especially in German.

[German : *um-*, around, alteration (from Middle High German *umb-*, from *umbe,* from Old High German *umbi*) + *Laut,* sound (from Middle High German *lūt,* from Old High German *hlūt*).]

🖙 The symbol ¨ is called an *umlaut* when it refers to change in the quality of a vowel, as in the German pair *Mann/Männer* ("man/men"), where the *a* is pronounced like the *a* in *father*, and the *ä* is pronounced like the *e* in *bet.* The same symbol is called a *dieresis* when it is placed over the second of two consecutive vowels, where it indicates that the two sounds are to be pronounced separately instead of as a diphthong, as in *Zoë* or *naïve.*

vi·cis·si·tude (vĭ-sĭs′ĭ-to͞od′, vĭ-sĭs′ĭ-tyo͞od′)

noun

A sudden or unexpected change of fortune; a variation in one's life, activities or situation: "*The aspect of the venerable mansion has always affected me like a human countenance, bearing the traces not merely of outward storm and sunshine, but expressive, also, of the long lapse of mortal life, and accompanying vicissitudes that have passed within*" (Nathaniel Hawthorne, *The House of the Seven Gables*).

[Latin *vicissitūdō,* from *vicissim,* in turn, probably from *vicēs,* plural of **vix,* change.]

vis·cer·al (vĭs′ər-əl)

adjective

1. Immediate and emotional; not deliberate or thought out: "*People are wary of Dag when meeting him for the first time, in the same visceral way prairie folk are wary of the flavor of seawater when tasting it for the first time at an ocean beach*" (Douglas Coupland, *Generation X*). **2.** Relating to, situated in, or affecting the viscera.

[Medieval Latin *vīscerālis:* Latin *vīscus,* plural *vīscera,* internal organs, innards + -*ālis,* adjectival suffix.]

vo·lup·tu·ous (və-lŭp**′**chōō-əs)

adjective

1. Characterized by or arising from sensual pleasure: *"Once in my room, I spread my clothes on my bed. The cufflinks were beaten up and had someone else's initials on them, but they looked like real gold, glinting in the drowsy autumn sun which poured through the window and soaked in yellow pools on the oak floor — voluptuous, rich, intoxicating"* (Donna Tartt, *The Secret History*). **2.** Sexually attractive, especially from having a curvaceous figure. **3.** Devoted to or indulging in sensual pleasures.

[Middle English, from Old French *voluptueux,* from Latin *voluptuōsus,* full of pleasure, from *voluptās,* pleasure.]

was·sail (wŏs**′**əl, wŏ-sāl**′**)

noun

1a. A salutation or toast given in drinking someone's health or as an expression of goodwill. **b.** The drink used in such toasting, commonly ale or wine spiced with roasted apples and sugar: *"When Duncan is asleep / . . . his two chamberlains / Will I with wine and wassail so convince / That memory, the warder of the brain, / Shall be a fume, and the receipt of reason / A limbeck only"* (William Shakespeare, *Macbeth*). **2.** A festivity characterized by much drinking: *"[L]ong had I nursed, in secret, the unnatural hatred—it blazed forth in an hour of drunken wassail"* (Walter Scott, *Ivanhoe*).

verb
> Past participle and past tense: **was·sailed**
> Present participle: **was·sail·ing**
> Third person singular present tense: **was·sails**

transitive To drink to the health of; toast.
intransitive To engage in or drink a wassail.

[Middle English, contraction of *wæshæil*, be healthy, from Old Norse *ves heill* : *ves,* imperative singular of *vera,* to be + *heill,* healthy.]

xer·o·phyte (zîr**′**ə-fīt**′**)

noun

A plant adapted to living in an arid habitat; a desert plant.

[From *xero-,* dry (from Greek *xēro-,* from *xēros*) + *-phyte,* plant (from Greek *phuton,* from *phuein,* to make grow).]

yogh (yŏg)

noun

The Middle English letter ȝ, used to represent the sound (y) and the voiced and voiceless velar fricatives.

[Middle English, possibly from Old English *īw, ēoh,* yew.]

ȝ In addition to the many grammatical differences and unfamiliar words, one of the things that modern readers find so difficult (or so charming) about Old and Middle English texts is the use of letters that have now become obsolete. These include yogh (ȝ), wynn or wen (ƿ), thorn (þ), edh (ð), and ash (æ). Yogh, originally the Old English form of the letter *g*, was used to represent several sounds, including the sound *ch* in Scottish *loch* that began to disappear from most varieties of English in the 1400s. The letters *y* or *gh* have replaced yogh in modern spelling. Wynn, which represented the sound (w), was borrowed by Old English scribes from the runes, the writing system of the early Germanic peoples. It was later superseded by the letter *w*, which was developed from two *u*'s or *v*'s written together. Both thorn (also a rune in origin) and edh were used indiscriminately to spell the two sounds (th) and *(th)*—the sounds in *breath* and *breathe*, respectively. The combination *th* now fills their role. Ash was used in Old English to represent the vowel (ă), as in the word *stæf*, meaning both "staff, stick of wood" and "letter (of the alphabet)." In this regard, it is interesting that several of the names for these old letters also relate to wood and trees, like *ash* and *thorn*. *Yogh* probably comes from Old English *īw* or *ēoh*, "yew tree."

Zeit·geist (tsīt′gīst′, zīt′gīst′)

noun

The spirit of the time; the taste and outlook character-istic of a period or generation: "*The prescription of psychoactive drugs for children has increased roughly threefold in the past decade, a particularly vivid demon-stration of the shift in the national Zeitgeist vis-à-vis psychological health*" (Arthur Allen, *Salon.com*).

[German : *Zeit,* time (from Middle High German *zīt,* from Old High German + *Geist,* spirit).]

ze·nith (zē′nĭth)

noun

1. The point on the celestial sphere that is directly above the observer: "*The sky stays clear, and when the sun reaches its zenith, I take a break and go down to the river*" (Sarah Pemberton Strong, *Burning the Sea*). **2.** The up-per region of the sky. **3.** The highest point above the observer's horizon attained by a celestial body. **4.** The point of culmination; the peak: *Her tenure as CEO was the zenith of her career.*

[Middle English *senith,* from Old French *cenith,* from Me-dieval Latin, from Arabic *samt* (*ar-ra's*), path (over the head), from Latin *sēmita,* path.]

The sky stays clear, and when the sun reaches its **zenith,** I take a break and go down to the river. The banks are always empty at noon. It's too hot to wash clothes, and all the cows are out grazing. In a few more hours, when the day will have cooled down, people will appear again to bathe, bringing pails to fill or leading their animals down to drink.

—Sarah Pemberton Strong,
Burning the Sea